Gu
Ham
the New Forest
Pub Walks

Ruth Paley

COUNTRYSIDE BOOKS
NEWBURY BERKSHIRE

First published 2023
© 2023 Ruth Paley

All rights reserved. No part of this publication may be reproduced,
stored in a retrieval system, or transmitted by any means, electronic,
mechanical, photocopying, recording or otherwise, without the prior
written permission of the copyright holder and publishers.

COUNTRYSIDE BOOKS
3 Catherine Road
Newbury, Berkshire

To view our complete range of books,
please visit us at
www.countrysidebooks.co.uk

ISBN 978 1 84674 424 2

All materials used in the production of this book carry FSC certification.

Cover image by Trevor Yorke
Produced by The Letterworks Ltd., Reading
Typeset by KT Designs, St Helens
Printed by Holywell Press, Oxford

Introduction

You will find all the ingredients for a successful walk in this guide. Rural Hampshire offers crystal-clear chalk streams, rolling downland, beech hangers and quaint villages with duck ponds, ancient churches and thatched cottages, as well as hedgerows and meadows humming with insect life, stunning vineyards and two National Parks.

On waterside walks by the Rivers Test, Meon and Itchen, look out for trout in the shallow waters, damselflies and, if you are very lucky, maybe otters. Try walk 8 in the Candover Valley, 6 in Longparish, 9 in Easton and 11 in East Meon. Walk 4 explores Greywell Moors Nature Reserve, an area of wet fenland fed by spring pools, before heading off along a stretch of the Basingstoke Canal.

Hampshire has many picturesque villages, with listed buildings, timber-framed cottages and welcoming pubs. Head to walk 5 in Amport, 6 in Longparish, 11 in East Meon and 13 in Buriton. Walk 1 in Highclere is also home to Highclere Castle, the filming location for *Downton Abbey*.

The chalk hills of the South Downs National Park run from the ancient cathedral city of Winchester and across Hampshire to Sussex. Walk 13 in Buriton, 11 in East Meon, and 12 in Steep all explore this rolling landscape, as well as being in an Area of Outstanding Natural Beauty.

Guide to Hampshire & the New Forest Pub Walks

Explore the New Forest and wander through ancient woods, heathlands and moor, where ponies, cattle and donkeys freely roam, in walk 15 in Fritham, 16 in Bolderwood, 17 in Rhinefield and 18 in Burley. Walk 14 lies on the western edge of the New Forest in Rockbourne, by the remains of a Roman Villa. Walk 19 takes you along coastal mudflats by Lymington, with views across the Solent. While in the New Forest, remember to keep your distance from the ponies and don't feed or pet them, also keep dogs on a lead. Be careful while driving as sadly around 50 ponies are killed by traffic every year.

All these walks have a pub on the route, or nearby. Please try and visit the pubs as you walk. The hospitality industry faced immense challenges during the pandemic, through lockdowns and restrictions. Pubs are at the heart of the community, and all the pubs in this book serve delicious food and welcome walkers. Check their website before setting off, to time your walk for when the kitchen is open.

Ruth Paley

Publisher's Note

We hope that you obtain considerable enjoyment from this book; great care has been taken in its preparation. Although at the time of publication all routes followed public rights of way or permitted paths, diversion orders can be made and permissions withdrawn.

We cannot, of course, be held responsible for such diversion orders or any inaccuracies in the text which result from these or any other changes to the routes, nor any damage which might result from walkers trespassing on private property. We are anxious, though, that all the details covering the walks are kept up to date, and would therefore welcome information from readers which would be relevant to future editions.

The simple sketch maps that accompany the walks in this book are based on notes made by the author whilst surveying the routes on the ground. They are designed to show you how to reach the start and to point out the main features of the overall circuit, and they contain a progression of numbers that relate to the paragraphs of the text.

However, for the benefit of a proper map, we do recommend that you purchase the relevant Ordnance Survey sheet covering your walk. Ordnance Survey maps are widely available, especially through booksellers and local newsagents.

1 Highclere

2½ miles / 4 km

WALK HIGHLIGHTS

This relaxing walk explores quiet country lanes in the North Wessex Downs, above the village of Highclere. After heading out through woods carpeted with snowdrops in winter, then bluebells in spring, the second half of the walk follows timeless lanes with wide verges filled with wild flowers and frothy cow parsley in summer. Through the hedgerows you can enjoy pastoral views across the downs and maybe glimpse deer in the meadows by the woods. The Red House is a friendly independent pub that welcomes walkers and dogs, note it's closed on Sundays and Mondays.

THE PUB

The Red House, Andover Road, Highclere, RG20 9PU.
☎ 01635 255531 ⊕ www.thehighclereredhouse.com

THE WALK

1 With your back to the **Red House**, turn right and walk a short distance to **Westridge**. Then turn right again and walk up the lane, with houses on your left and fields on your right. There is no pavement but there is very little traffic and there are wide grassy verges. Pass a turning on the left to Hollington and continue ahead, leaving the houses behind you now, until the lane turns sharply right.

Guide to Hampshire & the New Forest Pub Walks

START & PARKING: Park roadside with care at the bottom of Westridge, or if you are visiting the pub, the Red House has a large car park. **Sat Nav:** RG20 9PU.

MAP: OS Explorer 144 Basingstoke, Alton & Whitchurch and OS Explorer 158 Newbury & Hungerford. **Grid Ref:** SU435600.

TERRAIN: Mainly level with some uphill woodland walking, then easy walking along quiet country lanes. One stile with a dog sluice.

2 Where the lane turns, follow the wooden footpath sign directly ahead, over a stile. Walk downhill along a wide grassy path between hedgerows towards **Ireland's Copse**. Cross a small stream then go through a gap by the side of a gate into mixed copse with holly trees by the path.

3 The route winds through the woods heading gently uphill, with bluebells in spring. When you come to a post with a yellow **HCC arrow**, turn left. Pass a wooden board with arrows, and veer right down into a clearing.

4 The path heads left across a large meadow to a track and fingerpost. Turn right over a brook then veer diagonally left from the track and up into woods, following the yellow HCC arrow through the trees. A short uphill section takes you past tall pine trees.

5 Leave the woods and head into a large field. Follow the grassy path towards a metal farm gate with a narrow gap by its side and you will find yourself on **Hollington Lane**.

6 Turn left and walk down the country lane. This is easy walking with banks filled with wild flowers and cow parsley in spring and summer. The lane leads downhill, passing **Hollington Stud** and **Yews Old Farmhouse**, then uphill before levelling out to walk between fields and hedgerows. Eventually, you reach a Y-junction with a large field in front of you.

7 Turn left on **Hollington Lane**, passing red brick cottages, then open fields with **Pill Hill** steeply rising up on your right. At the junction with

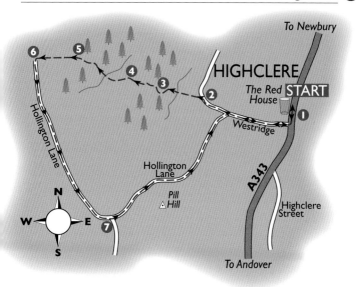

Westridge that you passed at the start of the walk, turn right and walk back down **Westridge**, then left to the **Red House**.

PLACES OF INTEREST NEARBY
Highclere Castle was built in 1679 and renovated in the 1840s by Sir Charles Barry, who also designed the Houses of Parliament, with parkland designed by Capability Brown in the 18th century. It is the country seat of the Earls of Carnarvon. The 5th Earl travelled to Egypt each year, after being advised by his doctor to avoid the damp English winters. In 1922, with Howard Carter, he discovered the tomb of Tutankhamun. Many of the treasures are displayed in an exhibition at the castle, and the Earl is buried on top of nearby Beacon Hill. Highclere Castle is also the filming location for **Downton Abbey**. For more information and entry tickets visit: www.highclerecastle.co.uk.

2 Kingsclere

2¾ miles / 4.4 km

WALK HIGHLIGHTS

Kingsclere lies on the edge of the North Wessex Downs, close to Watership Down. This easy walk starts at St Mary's church in the centre of the village. Have a look at the weathervane as you pass, legend has it that in the early 13th century, King John spent an uncomfortable night in a local inn due to bed bugs, and was so annoyed that he ordered a bed bug weathervane be made for the church. You leave the large churchyard via small footbridges over Well's Head, then head out into open countryside along the Brenda Parker Way, a long-distance path that crosses North Hampshire. The route rewards you with sweeping views towards Isle Hill and the North Hampshire Downs, before returning by arable fields to the village. The Crown is a tastefully decorated dog-friendly freehouse, opposite the church, serving good quality traditional food. For winter walkers there is a log fire, as well as plenty of tables outside to relax and watch village life during warmer weather.

START & PARKING: Anchor Road car park is free and clearly signed, opposite the church in the centre of the village. **Sat Nav:** RG20 5PQ.

MAP: OS Explorer 144 Basingstoke, Alton & Whitchurch.
   Grid Ref: SU526586.

TERRAIN: Level walking along chalk downland and arable fields with a small amount of road walking on quiet country lanes. Some wooden steps near the village.

THE PUB
The Crown, Newbury Road, Kingsclere, RG20 5QU.
☎ 01635 299500 ⊕ www.thecrownkingsclere.co.uk

THE WALK

❶ Follow the path through the churchyard to the far left corner, then cross the wide millstream. The narrow footpath leads you past gardens to **Fox's Lane**. Turn left along this quiet country lane. Just before **Bear Hill**, turn right to follow the **Brenda Parker Way** through a metal kissing gate (do not take the path to the right of 'Highcliffe' that leads diagonally up).

❷ Walk by the side of arable fields, admiring the views on your left towards **Isle Hill**. When you come to a large metal barn, turn right, following the **Brenda Parker Way** along a rutted farm track to **Ecchinswell Road**.

❸ Cross the road and turn right, walking along the wide verge. Pass **Frobury Farm**, then turn left, to follow the **Brenda Parker Way** along a narrow shady path.

❹ Look out for a small footpath post on your right, where you leave the long-distance path to follow the yellow arrows back towards **Kingsclere**. Walk by the side of a large arable field, then just before **Porch Farm**, turn right then left, passing the buildings on your left.

❺ Cross the field and walk through a wide gap in the hedge to another

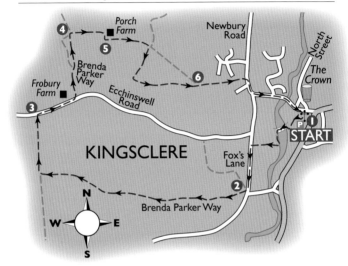

field. Turn right then left, to skirt the field until you come to a wooden post in the corner.

6 Follow the narrow path ahead past gardens and down some wooden steps and continue along '**Frogs Hole**' until you come to **Newbury Road**. Cross the road and turn right, then follow the pavement as it leads you round '**Corner House**' and back through the village to the **Crown pub** and the church.

PLACES OF INTEREST NEARBY

Sandham Memorial Chapel (National Trust) is five miles west, in Burghclere. This small chapel is home to large, evocative paintings by the British artist, Sir Stanley Spencer. The 19 canvases took six years to complete and depict various scenes from the First World War, when he served as a medical orderly and later as an infantryman. **Watership Down** is a steep hill 3 miles west of here, made famous as the setting for Richard Adams' novel.

3 **The Bourne Valley**
6 miles / 9.6 km

WALK HIGHLIGHTS
St Mary Bourne is a delightful village with many thatched cottages dating back to the 16th century, and the Bourne Rivulet. This tributary of the River Test is a seasonal chalk stream, rising in January and flowing until the dry summer months. The walk first explores St Mary Bourne Lake, excavated in the 1970s as a haven for wildlife and now popular for trout fishing. You then head gently uphill, by the side of large arable fields following the Brenda Parker Way, before taking the shady Long Hedge Drove with expansive views across this rural landscape to the North Wessex Downs. Return via Wadwick Bottom, then Wakes Wood, carpeted with bluebells and cowslips in spring. The George Inn is an attractive free house packed with character and welcomes dogs and walkers; definitely worth visiting at the end of the walk. The route follows some small country lanes, but once out of the village you could easily not see a single car.

THE PUB
The George Inn, St Mary Bourne, SP11 6BG.
☎ 01264 318000 ⊕ georgeinnstmarybourne.co.uk

THE WALK
1 With your back to the flint and stone church of **St Peter**, turn left

START & PARKING: The B3048 runs through the village, with the shop and free village car park signed down Bourne Meadow, almost opposite the pub. Otherwise, park roadside with care by the church.
Sat Nav: SP11 6BE.

MAP: OS Explorer 144 Basingstoke, Alton & Whitchurch.
Grid Ref: SU422503.

TERRAIN: Arable fields and quiet country lanes. Mainly level with no stiles. There are lots of paddocks by the walk so you might pass horse riders.

heading out of the village. Cross the road to follow the path on your right, signed to Derrydown.

2 Pass **St Mary Bourne Lake** and just past a house, turn right through a metal kissing gate to follow the **Test Way**. Veer diagonally across the recreation ground, heading for the gate just left of the hut. Continue along the footpath, crossing a small lane. When you come to **School Lane**, turn right and walk past the school to the main road.

3 Now turn left, then cross the road and turn right down **Gangbridge Lane** and walk by the side of the **Bourne Rivulet**.

4 Just past **Rowe Farm**, look out for a turning on your right and a purple footpath sign on your right. It is just before a yew hedge and **Monte Cristo house**. Now turn right to follow the **Brenda Parker Way** gently uphill, with lovely views across the Bourne valley.

5 When you get to the top of a field, with hedgerow in front of you, turn right then almost immediately left, through a gap in the hedge. There is a footpath arrow but it can be hard to spot. You are now following **Long Hedge Drove**. Continue along this ancient drovers' track in the same direction until you come to a surfaced lane and a footpath sign.

6 Turn right and just by **Overbourne House**, turn right to follow the footpath by the side of a field. The path continues left across an arable field, heading downhill, then through a gap in the hedge to **Wadwick Bottom**.

7 Turn right and follow the lane, passing a turning on your left to Egbury. Eventually, you come to double metal farm gates. Turn right by the gates to follow the Right of Way sign through **Wakes Wood**. When you come to a surfaced lane, turn left and walk down to the thatched **Butler's Farm**. Now turn left again and walk back through the village to the **George Inn**.

PLACES OF INTEREST NEARBY

Bourne Valley Pick Your Own (SP11 6DQ) is ½ mile outside the village and well worth a visit. As well as fruit picking, there's a farm shop, café, giant straw castle and children's playground. Check their website for opening times and updates on which crops are in season: www.bournevalleypyo.co.uk.

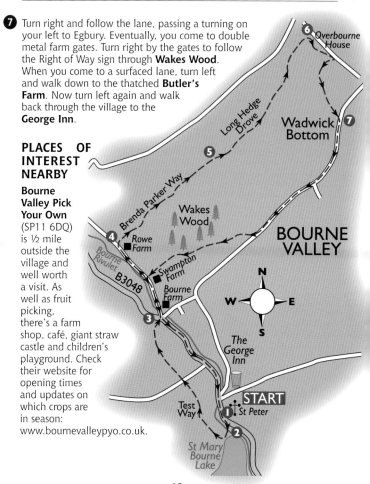

4 Greywell Moors

3 miles / 5 km

WALK HIGHLIGHTS

Greywell Moors Nature Reserve is an area of peaceful fen and woodland, with large pools attracting a range of different birds, as well as nationally rare orchids, ferns, mosses and liverworts. This walk also takes you past the entrance to Greywell Tunnel. This 1,120 metre tunnel led the Basingstoke Canal through Greywell Hill. The Basingstoke Canal was created in the 1780s, giving local farmers access to the London markets. The tunnel was dug by hand in candlelight, accessed via vertical shafts through the hill, then a tunnel dug in both directions from the bottom of each shaft. It has no towpath and boats had to be 'legged' through the dark, while the horses were walked over the top of the hill. Following various collapses, and the discovery of hibernating bats, there is now a locked gate to keep out boats and conserve one of Europe's largest bat roosts. As you walk along Basingstoke Canal, you also pass 13th-century Odiham Castle, before returning across meadows to the start.

START & PARKING: Follow Deptford Lane, then turn left for the turning to Greywell Water Treatment Works. There is space for a few cars here, just be careful not to block the gates. **Sat Nav:** RG29 1BS.

MAP: OS Explorer 144 Basingstoke, Alton & Whitchurch.
Grid Ref: SU722512.

TERRAIN: Level walking with boardwalks taking you over the water.

THE PUB
Fox and Goose, The Street, Greywell, RG29 1BY.
☎ 01256 702062 ⊕ www.facebook.com/foxandgoosegreywell

THE WALK

❶ Cross **Deptford Lane** and go through the metal gate into **Greywell Moors Nature Reserve**, following the bridleway across the wet fen. Follow the path through a metal gate. Stay on this path, through two metal kissing gates and past some water on your right. The path eventually turns right and leads down to a wooden fingerpost.

❷ Here you turn right and through a metal kissing gate to follow the footpath along the western edge of the nature reserve. Go through another kissing gate past the waters of **Spring Head** on your left. The path leads you past pretty **Greywell Mill**. Follow the footpath sign in front of the house, along a stretch of boardwalk over the banks of the **River Whitewater,** then into woodland.

❸ Cross the churchyard of **St Mary's church** and through the wooden gate into a large grassy area, with the cottages of **Greywell** over on your left. Walk ahead to the far right corner where a low stile leads you along a fenced path and back to **Deptford Lane**. Turning right here would take you back to your car.

❹ To continue the walk, turn left and walk almost up to the top of the lane and the **Fox and Goose pub**, then turn sharp right to follow the signed footpath which leads you over the **Greywell Tunnel** to the **Basingstoke Canal**. Turn right and follow the towpath. Pass a yellow footpath sign on your left, then **Odiham Castle**. Continue to the Lift Bridge and cross over the canal. Continuing along the lane ahead will lead you to the **Mill House pub**.

5 Turn right, now following the opposite bank of the canal for a short distance, before turning left back across the fen towards Greywell. Follow the footpath as it turns left, then right by an arable field. A rutted lane leads you back to **Deptford Lane**, where you turn right.

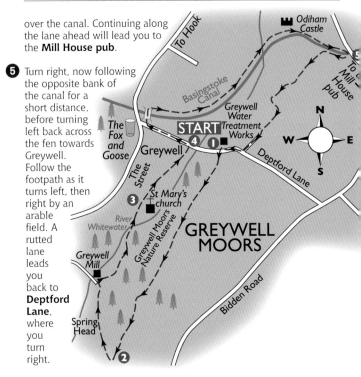

PLACES OF INTEREST NEARBY

Odiham Castle was built as a royal residence, but by the 15th century, it had been relegated to a hunting lodge, locals used it as a source of building material and by the 1600s it was a ruin. Just west of here is **Newlyns Farm Shop, Café and Cookery School** (RG29 1HA), the café welcomes dogs outside and the shop sells meat from their 500-acre farm, as well as a variety of local produce.

5 Amport & the Test Valley

4 miles / 6.4 km

WALK HIGHLIGHTS

Amport is a delightful conservation village with thatched cottages, a village green and willows by the chalk stream, Pillhill Brook. The walk offers sweeping views across the gently rolling downland of the Test Valley, and is a good choice for horse lovers, as you pass paddocks on the return journey. The Hawk Inn enjoys the perfect location, with plenty of space in front to sit and enjoy a drink in the meadow by Pillhill Brook, or relax in its wood-panelled interior, with dogs welcome throughout. Halfway round the walk you also pass the White Horse Inn, a thatched, Grade II listed free house.

THE PUB

The Hawk Inn, Amport, SP11 8AE.
☎ 01264 710371   ⊕ www.hawkinnamport.co.uk

THE WALK

1 Walk down to the main road, then turn right, passing the school, then right again down **Furzedown Lane**. Follow this no through road, passing massive yew trees, until you see 14th-century knapped flint **St Mary's Church** on your left. The footpath is directly opposite the church. Pass a garden then walk by the side of an arable field, until you see a small copse ahead.

Guide to Hampshire & the New Forest Pub Walks

START & PARKING: Start from the Green in the centre of the village, with an off-road parking area along its western edge.
  Sat Nav: SP11 8BA.

MAP: OS Explorer 131 Romsey, Andover & Test Valley.
  Grid Ref: SU302443.

TERRAIN: Mainly level. Field paths and some road walking. One stile.

2 Now veer right for a few metres, then continue ahead and downhill to an electric fence. Walk with the fence on your right to a gravel track. Keep in the same direction, following the track for about 100 metres, then turn right through a gate, following the yellow arrow.

3 Pass a thatched cottage to **Wiremead Lane**. Turn left and follow the lane through the village. Pass the sea scouts' hut on your right, then just before a turning to the left, with the **White Horse Inn** ahead of you, turn right to follow the public footpath.

4 Follow the narrow path until the hedge ends, then turn left and head straight across the field to a footpath sign on the other side. Now turn right, with the A303 on your left, to the end of the field. Turn right and follow the path for about 150 metres, then left through a gap in the hedge by a wooden post.

5 Walk ahead with a field on your left and a hedge on your right. Follow the field-edge to **Sarsen Lane**. Now turn right, then almost immediately left, crossing the road in front of 'Kimber' house to follow a narrow footpath between hedgerows. Ignore the stile on your right, and walk to the end of the path and a large arable field.

6 Turn right and follow the hedge round the field, turning right, then left. At the bottom of the field, turn right through a gap in the hedge and over a stile. Pass paddocks on your left and blackberry bushes on your right to the bottom of the paddock, and then turn right through a metal kissing gate. Follow the path past thatched cottages to the car park behind the **Hawk Inn**.

7 Cross the car park, turn right then left, to follow the restricted byway next to **Mill House**. Cross two small footbridges over the ford, then turn right by the edge of the fence to follow a footpath with a large house on your right. Go through a kissing gate and continue ahead. The footpath emerges by the side of **The Cottage on the Green**. Walk down the gravel drive and you will see the Green ahead of you.

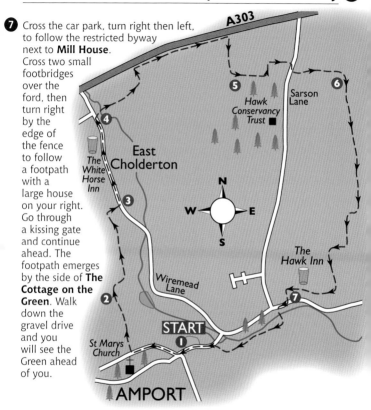

PLACES OF INTEREST NEARBY

The Hawk Conservancy Trust is less than a mile away. It has 150 birds of prey in 22 picturesque acres of woodland and wildflower meadows. Check their website for opening times, flying displays and the day's timetable: www.hawk-conservancy.org.

6 Longparish

3½ miles / 5.6 km

WALK HIGHLIGHTS

Exploring field paths north of the village, before walking by the banks of the River Test and alongside meadows. This is a good choice for late spring, when the meadows and hedgerows are filled with wild flowers and humming with life. Footbridges criss-cross the River Test and its tributaries as you walk. The Plough Inn was bought by the village as a community-owned pub. It has been lovingly brought back to life and serves excellent food.

THE PUB

The Plough Inn, Longparish, SP11 6PB.
☎ 01264 720069 ⊕ www.ploughinn.org

THE WALK

1 From the car park turn right, cross the road in front of the village hall and follow the footpath sign next to **Orchard House**. Follow the permissive footpath to the left, as it skirts round the garden of **Greenholme**, then continue ahead following the yellow footpath arrow into a playing field.

START & PARKING: Middleton is on the western edge of Longparish and there is free parking in the village car park opposite the graveyard. **Sat Nav:** SP11 6PB.

MAP: OS Explorer 144 Basingstoke, Alton & Whitchurch. **Grid Ref:** SU425439.

TERRAIN: Level walk and some roadside walking along quiet country lanes. There is one stile but you can bypass it with a nearby gate.

2 Cross the playing field, passing the beer garden of the **Plough** over on your right, and go through a gate marked 'public right of way'. The path leads between cottages to **Sugar Lane**. Turn left, then almost immediately right, to follow a footpath through a kissing gate into a large field. Follow the path through a kissing gate on the other side. Follow the path with fields on your left and copse on the right. Pass a footpath sign by a gate on your right, keeping ahead until you come to **North Acre**.

3 Turn left and follow the pavement, passing a footpath that leads off on your left. When the road leads sharply round to the left, follow the footpath ahead, next to number 132. The path leads between fields, crossing a track, then continues ahead into the next field, following a permissive footpath towards **East Aston** with the road on your right. At the end of the permissive path, walk ahead into the next field, along the footpath with the hedgerow on your left and the field on your right. Follow the path round the field, passing by the side of a wooden farm gate, then down a track to **Longparish Road** (B3048).

4 Turn left and walk roadside along the lane, passing **Mill House Lane** on your right. Look out for a footpath sign, then turn right and follow the footpath over a bridge, until another bridge takes you to a lane. Turn right and follow the lane to cross a bridge with **Upper Mill** ahead.

5 Turn left and follow the shady path by the banks of the **Test**, then over another footbridge to a grassy path with large meadows on your left. A long footbridge takes you back over the **Test**, and then through a kissing gate to a meadow. Veer slightly to the left and over a stile – if you have a dog there is a gate over on your right.

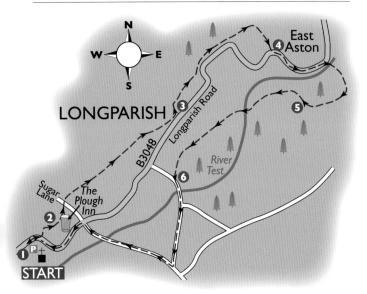

Walk across the centre of the field and then through a kissing gate. Continue ahead along a grassy path to the middle of the meadow and a fingerpost. Now veer left, following the footpath to a kissing gate and **Mill Lane**.

6 Turn left and follow **Mill Lane**. At the bottom of the lane, turn right onto **Southside Road**, crossing back over the **River Test**. Turn left at **Longparish Road**, passing the **Plough**. You could detour to look at **St Nicholas Church**, otherwise continue along the pavement to the car park on your left.

PLACES OF INTEREST NEARBY
Finkley Down Farm is open all year round, with animals, feeding activities and a play barn.

7 Upper & Lower Wield

3¼ miles / 5.2 km

WALK HIGHLIGHTS

Sleepy Upper Wield nestles by a village green with thatched cottages, a Norman church and Primitive Methodist Chapel. This peaceful walk across rolling downland, woods and farmland follows part of the Oxdrove Way, a 25-mile route that was once used as a drove route for cattle. It's a good choice for a sunny day, with much of the walk following shady hedgerows, passing the welcoming Yew Tree in Lower Wield in the middle of the walk. This delightful country pub lies opposite a cricket ground, with a large garden, open fire, beams and slate floor. It is dog-friendly and the food is excellent.

THE PUB

The Yew Tree, Lower Wield, SO24 9RX.
☎ 01256 389224   ⊕ www.theyewtreelowerwield.co.uk

THE WALK

1 From **Church Lane** walk back down to **Wield Road**, then turn right and walk to the signpost. Follow the road round to the left, signed

Guide to Hampshire & the New Forest Pub Walks

START & PARKING: Start from Church Lane where you'll find a small parking area, being careful not to block any drives. To visit the church, follow the footpath sign on the right. **Sat Nav:** SO24 9RT.

MAP: OS Explorer 132 Winchester, New Alresford & East Meon. **Grid Ref:** SU629387.

TERRAIN: Level walking with some road walking in Upper Wield. One stile but with a gate next to it. Could be muddy after rain. Lots of opportunities for dogs to be safely off lead.

Lower Wield and Medstead. Pass the 1876 red brick village hall and continue ahead, out of the village. Ignore a turn on the right, and after ½ mile you come to a T-junction.

2 Cross the road and follow **Oxdrove Way**, passing the side of a metal farm gate. The route starts as a gravel track between hedgerows, then walk under trees with views across the fields for about a mile. When you meet a cross path with a footpath sign, turn left. The byway leads gently uphill, then levels out for a peaceful shady stretch. You eventually come to a metal five-bar gate and a road (**Ashley Road**).

3 Turn left along the road then right, following the sign for Lower Wield. Shortly you will see the large yew tree outside the pub on your right. Pass the pub and walk uphill, past thatched cottages, and just next to **Drove Cottage** turn left, following the footpath sign.

4 The path leads you along a grassy path under trees. Go through a metal kissing gate and straight across an arable field, following the line of telegraph poles. When you come to a hedge, there is a choice of paths. Go through the hedge and straight ahead, through a gate to walk by the side of paddocks, then by a gate to follow a track.

5 The track ends with a stile, but you can go through the farm gate if it's easier. Turn left and follow the road back into **Upper Wield**, passing the impressive thatched **Old Post Cottage**, and **Wield Manor**. Turn right at the sign for the church to return to your car.

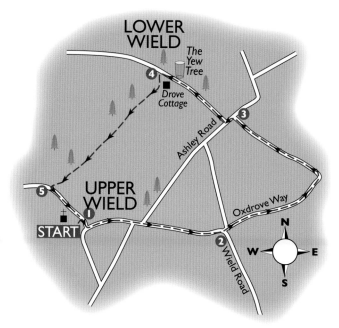

PLACES OF INTEREST NEARBY

The walk takes you almost past the door of **Hattingley Valley Winery**, in Lower Wield. They have a 600-tonne capacity winery and offer a step-by-step guide to how they produce their award-winning sparkling wine. There's also the opportunity to buy their wine at cellar door prices if you like what you've tasted. To book a tour and tasting experience visit their website:hattingleyvalley.com. West of here is **Chawton**, home to the 18th-century novelist Jane Austen for the last eight years of her life. Jane and her sister, Cassandra, used to walk every day through this countryside. The house where she lived is now a museum, celebrating her life, works and legacy: janeaustens.house

8 Candover Valley

3 miles / 4.8 km

WALK HIGHLIGHTS

This easy walk follows a stretch of the 70-mile long-distance walking route, the Wayfarer's Walk, through the rural chalklands of central Hampshire in the valley of the Itchen. Starting at the Woolpack Inn, follow this ancient droving route, used for hundreds of years to herd cattle and sheep to market, with sweeping views across the countryside to the picturesque hamlet of Brown Candover. Here you follow the clear waters of Candover Brook, a chalk steam and tributary of the River Itchen, perfect for four-legged walking companions. The stream meanders through the meadows taking you back to the pub. The stream is also one of the few remaining homes of the endangered native white-clawed crayfish. The Woolpack is a popular pub with plenty of space inside or in its garden. It's dog-friendly and serves locally sourced food, including trout and watercress from the local chalk streams.

THE PUB

The Woolpack Inn, Totford, SO24 9TJ.
☎ 01962 734184 ⊕ www.thewoolpackinn.co.uk

START & PARKING: The Woolpack Inn has a large car park, but make sure you visit the pub and check with the landlord as a courtesy. **Sat Nav:** SO24 9TJ.

MAP: OS Explorer 132 Winchester, New Alresford & East Meon. **Grid Ref:** SU571379.

TERRAIN: Mainly level easy walking, with most of the walk along surfaced tracks.

THE WALK

1 Directly to the right of the **Woolpack Inn**, follow the **Wayfarer's Walk** as it heads gently uphill, passing stables, then straight on between hedgerows. After nearly a mile, the path emerges at the bottom of a farm track. Turn right, and walk past large metal barns to the fingerpost sign.

2 Now turn left and follow the restricted byway along **Spybush Lane**, admiring the sweeping views across the Candovers. Cross the clear waters of Candover chalk stream to the B3046.

3 Turn left and walk through the village of **Brown Candover**, following the wide verge. Cross the road by the village sign and leave the main road to follow the signed **Wayfarer's Walk**. The stream goes under the road then continues to the left of your path.

4 When the surfaced lane veers right, continue straight ahead, following the signed bridleway and **Wayfarer's Walk**, passing gardens then

fields on either side of you. The stream eventually veers off to the left across the meadows, but continue ahead along the path, passing Totford Farm down on your left.

5 When you come to the road, turn left and walk roadside by this quiet country lane, to return to the pub and the start of the walk.

PLACES OF INTEREST NEARBY

Travel by steam along the heritage **Watercress Line** through 10 miles of Hampshire countryside, from the Georgian town of Alresford to Alton. A stop off at Ropley offers a chance to see the engines and carriages being restored. The line was originally used to transport locally grown watercress from Hampshire's chalk streams to London markets. A ticket will let you hop on and off the line for the day: watercressline.co.uk. Children will enjoy **Winchester Science Centre and Planetarium**, as it brings science, technology, engineering and maths to life through a variety of hands-on interactive exhibits spread over two floors. It also has a large and very impressive planetarium, taking you on a tour through space.

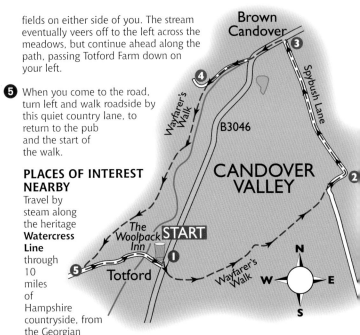

9 **Easton & the River Itchen**

3½ miles / 5.6 km

WALK HIGHLIGHTS

A waterside walk through the Itchen Valley by the edge of the South Downs National Park, starting at Easton's Norman church, dating from the 12th century. The route follows field paths, woodland tracks and riverside trails, with plenty of opportunities to admire the sparkling waters of the River Itchen. This beautiful chalk stream flows through Hampshire to Southampton and is a designated Site of Special Scientific Interest. The riverbanks are home to water voles, otters and white-clawed crayfish, the UK's only native freshwater crayfish; while kingfishers, butterflies and dragonflies dart over the water. Much of this walk follows the 28-mile Itchen Way, with several points where you cross the water via wooden footbridges. You also follow St Swithun's Way, part of the medieval pilgrims' route to the shrine of St Thomas Becket in Canterbury from Winchester. The water and lack of roads make this an excellent choice for dog walkers.

Guide to Hampshire & the New Forest Pub Walks

START & PARKING: Follow the main road through the village and park roadside by the church on Church Lane, a no through road.
   Sat Nav: SO21 1EN.

MAP: OS Explorer 132 Winchester, New Alresford & East Meon.
   Grid Ref: SU509321.

TERRAIN: Level walking with one stile, with easy access for even a large breed dog, some wooden footbridges and about 20 metres by the side of the B3047 along a wide grass verge.

THE PUB
The Chestnut Horse, Easton, SO21 1EG.
☎ 01962 779300   ⊕ www.thechestnuthorse.com

THE WALK
1 From the church, turn right and just past **Church Cottage**, follow the yellow footpath arrow diagonally across the village recreation ground and through a kissing gate. The path leads across a field and over a stile. You will soon see reeds by the **River Itchen**, then a shady stretch as the route takes you under trees. Cross a footbridge over the Itchen, then a subway under the M3. Follow the path until you come to gravel parking and **Long Walk**.

2 Turn right over a footbridge, passing **Fulling Mill**. A series of small footbridges lead you across meadows and through a metal kissing gate, until you come to an information board on **Mill Lane**, by **Abbots Worthy**. Walk ahead past **Abbotsworthy Mill**, before turning right through a metal kissing gate.

3 Follow the **Itchen Way**, taking the left fork away from the river. The path leads up to the B3047, where you turn right along the grass verge in front of a flint-walled house, then right to return to the footpath. The route takes you back under the M3, then through metal kissing gates and across fields until you come to **Easton Lane**.

4 Cross the lane and follow the footpath to **Martyr Worthy** (a right turn at Easton Lane would take you back to the village, but you would miss

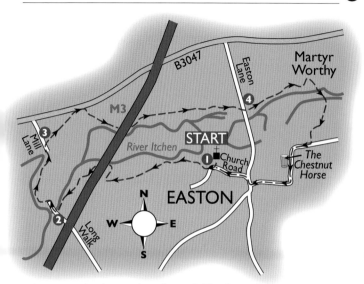

out on some lovely stretches of water). The footpath emerges onto a lane by a chocolate-box thatched cottage. Turn right and follow the **Itchen Way** over a long footbridge with idyllic views along the river. Continue over smaller footbridges and a field. Veer right through a metal gate, then walk down the footpath to a lane. Now turn right and head back through the village, passing the **Chestnut Horse**. Turn left up **Church Lane**.

PLACES OF INTEREST NEARBY

Winchester, England's ancient capital and former seat of King Alfred the Great, is definitely worth visiting. You can easily visit all the main sites on foot, and there are plenty of shops, restaurants and cafés to keep everyone happy. The 11th-century cathedral is the resting place of Jane Austen, the atmospheric 13th-century Great Hall houses King Arthur's Round Table, while the City Mill is one of the oldest working watermills in the country.

10 Horsebridge & King's Somborne

2¾ miles / 4.4 km

WALK HIGHLIGHTS

This walk starts with a shady stretch along the Monarch's Way, the escape route taken by King Charles II in 1651, after his defeat at the Battle of Worcester. The path was also the track of the Sprat and Winkle railway line, which closed in the 1960s. The River Test has a mass of tributaries, and although much of the riverbank is fenced off for fishing, the start of the walk offers good views across chalk streams. Head off across the Hampshire Downs to King's Somborne, then back by fields and by gardens to Horsebridge.

THE PUB

The John O'Gaunt Inn, Horsebridge, SO20 6PU.
☎ 01794 388644 ⊕ www.johnofgaunt.co.uk

THE WALK

1 From the parking spot on **Horsebridge Road**, turn left to follow the **Test Way/Monarch's Way** signed towards **Inkpen Beacon**. Cross a footbridge over a tributary of the Test and continue ahead enjoying the sound of running water and birdsong.

START & PARKING: There are parking spaces either side of Horsebridge Road at the start of the walk, by the Monarch's Way/Test Valley footpath sign. There's also a small car park if you follow the lane opposite the pub, signed to Horsebridge Station. There is no parking at the pub. **Sat Nav:** SO20 6PU.

MAP: OS Explorer 131 Romsey, Andover & Test Valley.
Grid Ref: SU344304.

TERRAIN: One downhill section on a field path that can be muddy after rain.

2 After ¾ mile, you come to a junction of footpaths. Turn right, leaving the **Test Way** to follow the **Clarendon Way** slightly uphill along a surfaced track. Pass **How Park Barn** and **Farm** on your left, to come to a corner of a surfaced lane, with metal farm gates on your left. Walk ahead to the footpath sign and turn right to follow the footpath.

3 This narrow path heads downhill between hedgerows, with a tapestry of fields ahead of you and skylarks in the fields. Cross a footbridge over **Somborne Stream** then pass a thatched cottage to **Romsey Road**.

4 Cross the road and turn right, then almost immediately left, to follow a footpath next to **Wattle Cottages**. Follow the path between gardens, then along the edge of the recreation ground and through a wide gap in the hedge into a large field with the 12th-century parish church over on your left. Turn right, passing a sign for the 'Trail End' and a bench, then right next to a five-bar gate, to follow the footpath back across the recreation ground, passing behind the goal posts. If you are feeling particularly energetic, there is a trail of exercise challenges round this field.

5 Leave the recreation ground by the side of a wooden gate then follow the short path by a hedge to **Palace Close**. Cross the road and turn right, heading back towards **Romsey Road**, but before reaching the road, turn left to follow a narrow footpath between hedges and fences, which brings you out by a bend further along **Romsey Road**.

6 Cross the road with care, and go through a metal kissing gate by the side

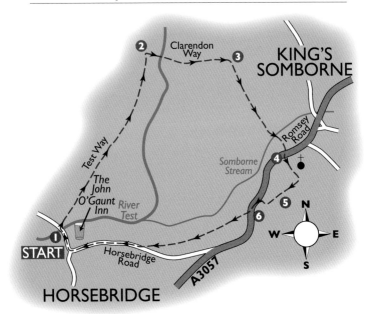

of a metal five-bar gate, just to the right of **Meadow Brook**. There are two footpath signs ahead of you, take the one on the right, then walk across the field, and through a metal kissing gate on the other side. Now follow a series of metal gates, as the footpath takes you across fields and through the backs of gardens. Dogs will need to be on a lead for this stretch. A final kissing gate leads you back to **Horsebridge Road**. Turn right, then right again to pass the **John O'Gaunt pub** and the mill to return to your car.

PLACES OF INTEREST NEARBY

The National Trust's 18th-century **Mottisfont House** is 3 miles from here (SO51 0LP), known for its stunning collection of roses, medieval priory and riverside gardens. Dogs on a lead are welcomed in the garden.

11 East Meon

3½ miles / 5.6 km

WALK HIGHLIGHTS

East Meon is a delightful village in the heart of the South Downs National Park, with two attractive pubs to choose from, The Izaak Walton and Ye Olde George Inn. The walk leads you east of the village through Greenway Copse, with panoramic views up to Park Hill. The return route explores peaceful village lanes by the clear, shallow waters of the River Meon. The River Meon is a chalk stream, with its source at East Meon. It runs for 21 miles through the Meon Valley to the Solent, and is renowned for its fly fishing.

THE PUB

The Izaak Walton, East Meon, GU32 1QA.
☎ 01730 823252   ⊕ www.theizaakwalton.com

THE WALK

1 Walk out of the car park, and straight ahead through the gap in the hedge next to the gate, and across the green. The footpath runs between the new houses directly ahead. Veer right across a paved area to

Guide to Hampshire & the New Forest Pub Walks

START & PARKING: Free parking at East Meon car park off Workhouse Lane, at the western edge of the village. **Sat Nav:** GU32 1PF.

MAP: OS Explorer OL32 Winchester, New Alresford & East Meon. **Grid Ref:** SU677222.

TERRAIN: Mainly level with some road walking, pavements and field paths. Sheep in some of the fields. A short stretch along a sunken off-road cycle track will be muddy after rain.

Duncombe Road. Walk up the road, then left along **Coombe Road**. Ignore a footpath sign on the right, and follow the pavement downhill to the village school. Cross the road and head up **Temple Lane**, then at the top, bear right along **Anvil Close**.

2 Go through a metal kissing gate to follow the public footpath across a meadow, with views on your right across the South Downs. Go through a metal gate and down to the road. Turn left and follow the road for about 100 metres. At the junction of **High Street** and **Frogmore Lane**, turn right through the gate to follow a footpath diagonally across the cricket pitch and through the metal gate on the other side. Follow the path ahead between fences, and continue, crossing a track, until you come to a metal farm gate on your right.

3 Turn right, following the footpath with a hedge on your left. Go through a kissing gate and continue along the path. Go through a wooden kissing gate and across a meadow, heading towards the pylons (there are sometimes sheep in this field). Go through the wooden kissing gate on the other side to **Frogmore Lane**.

4 Cross the road and take the track directly in front of you, ignoring the path on your left leading up to a metal gate. Follow this track, eventually passing, on your left, the metal gates of a very remote house. Go ahead, past a metal gate and posts until you come to a junction of paths. Now turn left, then shortly left again, following a byway and passing paddocks on your right.

5 At **East Meon Road**, opposite **Rookham Lodge**, turn left and walk

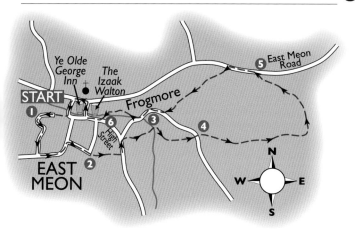

roadside with care, past the bus stop and under pylons. Just past the pink house, **Germans Barn**, turn left to follow a narrow sunken path, signed as an off-road cycle track. This leads you back to **Frogmore**, where you turn right to head back towards **East Meon**. At a small bridge, turn right and follow the footpath with first the **Meon** on your left, then some allotments. Stay on this surfaced path as it curves left, and leads you down to the **High Street**.

6 Turn right, passing the **Isaak Walton pub**. Continue along the road to **Ye Olde George Inn**, where you turn right and pass 19th-century almshouses. Walk to **All Saints' Church** and turn left to the end of the church wall, then left by the pink house, **Vicarage Lodge**, to walk down **The Cross**. Turn right down **Workhouse Lane**, passing the village hall on your left, to the car park.

PLACES OF INTEREST NEARBY

The National Trust's **Hinton Ampner** (SO24 0NH) has a magnificent house and gardens with sculptured topiary, rose gardens and views across the South Downs countryside. There is also a café in the former stable block.

12 Steep & Ashford Stream

4¼ miles / 6.8 km

WALK HIGHLIGHTS

This walk starts by a quirky pub, unlike any other pub you will visit. The Harrow Inn has been in the same family since 1932 and is run by two sisters, both born and brought up in the pub. It has won numerous awards, been included in the *Good Beer Guide* every year since it was published, and its cheddar ploughman's is ranked number 321 in the *Lonely Planet's Ultimate Eatlist – the World's Top 500 Food Experiences*. The peaceful walk in an Area of Outstanding Natural Beauty explores meadows, woods and streams near rural Steep, with panoramic views towards Ashford Hangers Nature Reserve.

THE PUB

The Harrow Inn, Steep, GU32 2DA.
☎ 01730 262685 ⊕ www.harrowinnsteep.co.uk
NOTE: payment by cash or cheque only.

THE WALK

1 Pass the pub on your left and walk down to the bottom of the lane, then left over a footbridge following **Shipwrights Way**. Turn left and follow the path past a timber-framed cottage, by **Ashford Stream**. The path leads you to a bend on the corner of **Sandy Lane**.

2 Turn left and head uphill, passing **Kettlebrook Stream**. Opposite **Tower Cottage**, turn left to follow a footpath, with stables on your right. Go

38

START & PARKING: There is limited space outside the pub, so please don't park between 12-3 pm unless you are eating in the pub. There is some parking along Harrow Lane. **Sat Nav:** GU32 2DA.

MAP: OS Explorer OL33 Petersfield. **Grid Ref:** SU751251.

TERRAIN: Some uphill and downhill sections, woodland paths, fields and village lane walking. There are stiles but all are accessible for dogs. There can be sheep and cattle on this walk.

through a gate on your left, or over the stile, then walk ahead across the field towards the woods. Cross the stile and the path leads you left, then steeply downhill through the woods.

3 Shortly you come to a cross path where you turn right. The path leads gently uphill, then levels out through **The Moors** woods. Cross a stile and continue ahead, crossing the drive of **Taylors Copse Cottage**. Pass wood sheds and continue ahead over a stile. Pass a large grain store on your right, and cross the footbridge, then over a stile. Follow the line of trees, with the field on your left, to cross another stile. The path now leads up to a kissing gate, where you follow the line of telegraph poles across a sloping pasture, heading towards trees. Go through a kissing gate, then up the path by the edge of trees, with a steep drop on your right. Continue ahead to **Mill Lane**.

4 Turn left along this quiet lane as it winds back towards **Steep**. Directly opposite **Island Farm Road**, turn left to follow **Hangers Way** through a kissing gate.

5 The path leads you round a meadow. Cross a bridge and through a kissing gate into **Northfield Wood**. At a bench and noticeboard, turn right then walk across the school field towards **All Saints Church**. Turn left just before the road, taking the permissive path by telegraph poles. The path leads downhill, through a kissing gate, then left across a field. Go through two kissing gates to walk between garden fences. Cross the drive to **The Grange** then **Steep Farm**, then left along a tarmac drive, left again and downhill, following a footpath arrow. Cross a bridge and you find yourself back at the path from point 3.

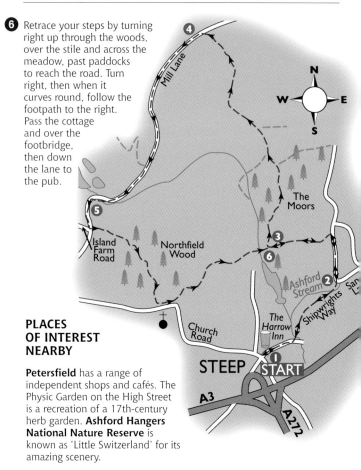

6 Retrace your steps by turning right up through the woods, over the stile and across the meadow, past paddocks to reach the road. Turn right, then when it curves round, follow the footpath to the right. Pass the cottage and over the footbridge, then down the lane to the pub.

PLACES OF INTEREST NEARBY

Petersfield has a range of independent shops and cafés. The Physic Garden on the High Street is a recreation of a 17th-century herb garden. **Ashford Hangers National Nature Reserve** is known as 'Little Switzerland' for its amazing scenery.

13 Buriton
2½ miles / 4 km

WALK HIGHLIGHTS
Buriton has an idyllic setting, with village pond, Norman church and Grade II listed pub. It is also in the South Downs, with this walk following part of the South Downs Way exploring chalk grassland, hangers and ancient drovers' paths. Although you are very near Butser Hill, the highest point of the South Downs, the walk is mainly level. You start by Buriton Chalk Pits. Now a local nature reserve, the area was quarried from the 1860s to the Second World War, when it was used for enemy mine disposal. The path follows the old narrow-gauge railway lines that were used to move the chalk and lime, before you head out into open downland with panoramic views across the Western Weald of the South Downs.

THE PUB
The Five Bells, Buriton, GU31 5RX.
☎ 01730 263584 ⊕ www.fivebells-buriton.co.uk

Guide to Hampshire & the New Forest Pub Walks

START & PARKING: Drive through the village to St Mary's church where there is a small parking area. **Sat Nav:** GU31 5RT. Alternatively, Halls Hill Car Park in Kiln Lane is at point 3 of the walk. **Sat Nav:** GU31 5SJ.

MAP: OS Explorer OL33 Haslemere & Petersfield and OL8 Chichester. **Grid Ref:** SU739200.

TERRAIN: The walk is mainly level, with only short up or downhill sections. Grassy paths and surfaced tracks.

THE WALK

1 From the church, cross the bridge over the village pond and turn left down **South Lane**, following the sign for **Hangers Way**. You pass a small graveyard and thatched cottages, before the surfaced lane turns into a track and heads up into trees and under a railway bridge. Continue ahead and gradually uphill, following the bridleway and admiring the ferns in the steep banks by the path.

2 Pass a sign for **Buriton Chalk Pits nature reserve** and a steep path leading up on your left, and continue ahead with a wire fence on your right. There is an information board here giving you the history of the chalk pits and limeworks. There's a short uphill section, and another side track leading into the chalk pits that you ignore. Follow the path, passing another information board to arrive at **Kiln Lane** with **Hall Hill car park** opposite you.

3 Join a section of the **South Downs Way**. Turn left, passing a 'no through road' and follow the surfaced lane. The route heads uphill, levels off, then downhill, passing a cottage on your right. Continue ahead following a track with fields on your left, still on the South Downs Way. Eventually you pass **Coulters Dean Farm** on your right, and continue ahead to a wooden fingerpost sign by the entrance to **Coulters Dean nature reserve**.

4 Turn left, following the **South Downs Way** for a short distance until you come to a wooden fingerpost on your left.

5 Turn left to follow a public byway known as the **Milky Way** due to the

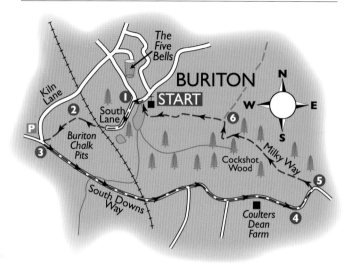

milky white chalkiness of the ground. This shady path leads you downhill through **Cockshot Wood**.

6 When you come to metal farm gates on either side of you, turn left through the kissing gate to follow the grassy footpath back towards **Buriton**, with grassland on your left leading up to hangers of ancient beech, lime, yew and ash woodland, a good spot for spotting deer. Pass some cottages on your right, before going through a kissing gate to return to the car park and the church.

PLACES OF INTEREST NEARBY

Nearby **Queen Elizabeth Country Park** (PO8 0QE) has 2,000 acres of downland and woodland. There are two cycle trails and three walking trails, as well as an assault course and dog activity centre to challenge your four-legged friend. Children can enjoy an adventure play area, an animal themed play park for younger children and there's also a café.

14 Rockbourne

5½ miles / 8.4 km

WALK HIGHLIGHTS

Rockbourne lies on the edge of Cranborne Chase, an AONB offering rolling chalk grassland, ancient woodlands and chalk river valleys. This walk is a good choice for history and horse lovers, as there is a Roman villa and museum in Rockbourne, and stables and racehorses in Whitsbury. The route leads round Whitsbury Castle ditches, although the earthworks are on private land, public footpaths encircle all but the eastern edge. The return offers sweeping views across Dunberry Hill towards the West Wiltshire Downs. The Rose and Thistle in Rockbourne and the Cartwheel in Whitsbury, are both excellent traditional pubs, but note both are closed on Mondays and the Rose and Thistle also on Thursdays.

THE PUB

Rose and Thistle, Rockbourne, SP6 3NL.
☎ 01725 518236 ⊕ www.roseandthistle.co.uk

THE WALK

1 Take the footpath opposite the village hall, signed to the church. Cross a footbridge over **Sweatfords Water** and walk to the church, where you turn right in front of it, then left by the side of the graveyard. Continue ahead and slightly uphill, under the trees. Meet a cross path and continue ahead, following the footpath. The path ends at an arable field, where you turn right, then left, to cross the field. Turn left on the

START & PARKING: There is a small parking space just past the Rose and Thistle pub, and before the village hall. **Sat Nav:** SP6 3NL.

MAP: OS Explorer OL22 New Forest. **Grid Ref:** SU113183.

TERRAIN: Field paths, some road walking, gentle ups and downs.

other side, then through a metal kissing gate on your right. Walk straight ahead along a ridged track and down to the road.

2 Turn left out of **Whitsbury**, passing stables on the left. Just after **Whitsbury Manor Stud**, follow the sign ahead for the bridleway and racing stables. Veer right round the brick stables, then straight ahead, ignoring a path heading left. Go through a metal farm gate and follow the grassy path, with the castle ditches through the trees on your right. At the end of this path, turn right onto **Long Steeple Lane**. Follow this grassy path, passing the drive to **Down Farm** on your left.

3 When you come to a wide gate on your right by a footpath post, go through the smaller gate and head towards **Lower Farm**. The footpath leads straight through the centre of the farmyard so keep your dog on a lead. There is a painted footpath arrow on the brick wall, showing the direction of the footpath. Continue straight on to follow the clearly signed footpath along a drive, with paddocks either side. Where the drive ends, continue ahead into the trees.

4 At a cross track turn right, and as you walk you will see **St Leonards church** on your left. Walk by a paddock and when you come to a bungalow, turn right to follow the signed footpath. This path leads straight ahead, then veers left to the church. Turn right through a small gate to follow the path through the graveyard, then take the footpath on your right, opposite the oak church doors.

5 Walk downhill, passing a manor house, then a thatched cottage until you reach the road. Turn left then just before **Lower Grove**, with the **Cartwheel Inn** ahead, turn right, following the public footpath sign.

6 This narrow path leads behind gardens and paddocks, and through a

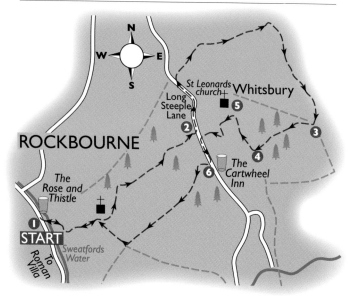

metal gate by an arable field. Cross a bridleway and continue ahead, with lovely views across the rolling landscape. Walk down a wide grassy path and look out for a metal gate on your right. Turn right through the gate and follow a narrow footpath between hedges. Ignore any side turnings and continue along the path, passing the village school, until you return to the church in **Rockbourne**. Now retrace your steps back to the village.

PLACES OF INTEREST NEARBY
Rockbourne Roman Villa (SP6 3PG) is open Thursday to Sunday, 11 am to 4 pm, and closes from October to April. The archaeological site has the remains of a Roman mosaic and the museum explores Roman life.

15 Fritham

3 miles / 4.8 km

WALK HIGHLIGHTS

This walk takes you right into the heathland following grassy tracks, with lots of opportunities to admire the New Forest ponies. The route starts by the village green in picturesque Fritham, by the thatched Royal Oak pub, named after the ancient oak tree opposite. Eyeworth Pond near the start of the walk is a peaceful spot for a picnic, this man-made gunpowder mill pond was created in the 1880s, with its remote location chosen to limit damage if an unexpected explosion occurred. The thatched Royal Oak dates back to the 17th century and is one of the oldest pubs in the New Forest. It is dog-friendly and a popular spot for walkers, serving homemade and locally-sourced food, note it's closed on Mondays and Tuesdays.

THE PUB

The Royal Oak, Fritham, SO43 7HJ.
☎ 0238 0812606 ⊕ www.royaloakfritham.co.uk

THE WALK

1 With your back to the car park, turn left and walk by the side of the road into the woods. The road leads you gently downhill through **Howen Bushes** to **Eyeworth Pond**.

Guide to Hampshire & the New Forest Pub Walks

START & PARKING: There is a free forestry commission car park just past the pub, next to the village green. **Sat Nav:** SO43 7HL.

MAP: OS Explorer OL22 New Forest. **Grid Ref:** SU230140.

TERRAIN: Heathland and tracks, mainly level, no gates or stiles.

2 Turn right, passing the pond on your left and the car park on your right, then walk by the wooden barrier gate and follow the path ahead across the heathland of **Howen Bottom**. The path gradually leads you uphill and as you can see the road ahead, veers left. Look out for a grass cross track near some silver birch trees.

3 Here turn right and follow the slightly rutted grass track across the heath.

4 The next turning is easy to miss. Look out for a wide grassy path about a quarter of the way across the common, with gorse bushes either side. Here you turn right, along **Longcross Plain** towards the trees of **Howen Bushes** in the distance.

5 When you get to the woodland, veer left and walk between the trees with a wire stock fence on your left. The path joins a rutted track. Continue ahead until you pass **Howen Farm**. You will then see the village green ahead where you turn left for the pub, or right to return to your car.

PLACES OF INTEREST NEARBY

The iron-clad **Rufus Stone** marks the spot where King William II was fatally wounded with an arrow, during a royal hunting trip in 1100 AD. The parking area is just south of the Sir Walter Tyrrell pub (SO43 7HD), or a 5 minute walk from the pub. **Furzey Gardens** (SO43 7GL) is a woodland garden with a thatched tea room, unusual plants and 40 fairy doors to spot on your way round. The gardens and tea rooms are open every day, 10am – 4pm. For animal lovers, head to the **New Forest Wildlife Park**, off the A35 between Southampton and Lyndhurst. Many of the animals are on the IUCN endangered list, and the park helps breed and conserve them for the future, as well as rehabilitating

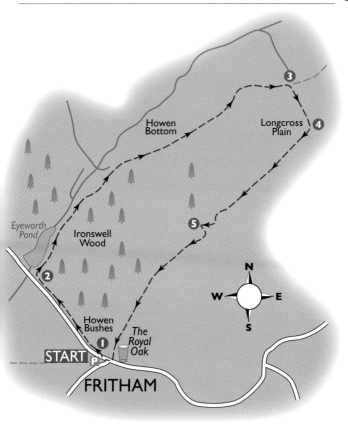

injured and orphaned native species, running a harvest mouse captive breeding programme and working with the RSPCA to rescue injured and abandoned wild animals: newforestwildlifepark.co.uk.

16 Bolderwood Deer Sanctuary

3 miles / 4.8 km

WALK HIGHLIGHTS

This walk guarantees you'll see deer, with a purpose-built platform overlooking a meadow where deer are fed daily near the start of the walk. Large information panels help you to identify the five different types of deer found in the New Forest: red, fallow, roe, sika and muntjac. Dusk and dawn are the best times to spot these shy creatures, although your chances on this walk are high, as after walking through woods and heathland, you pass Bolderwood Deer Sanctuary. The walk also explores military history, passing the Canadian Memorial, commemorating World War Two Canadian forces stationed in the New Forest before the D-Day invasion in 1944. This is an easy-to-navigate walk in the heart of the New Forest, through woodland, open moors and heath. The popular New Forest Inn is a 5 minute drive away, as you head towards Lyndhurst.

THE PUB

The New Forest Inn, Emery Down, SO43 7DY.
☎ 023 8028 4690 ⊕ www.thenewforestinn.co.uk

THE WALK

1 From the car park, go through the gate next to the map and follow the

START & PARKING: Bolderwood Car Park, next to Bolderwood Deer Sanctuary, is a large free car park with toilets, a picnic spot and often an ice cream van. **Sat Nav:** SO43 7GQ.

MAP: OS Explorer OL22 New Forest. **Grid Ref:** SU242086.

TERRAIN: Gravel tracks and some gentle uphill stretches. Keep dogs on a lead to protect the deer. This walk could easily be done with an all terrain pushchair.

yellow posts, crossing a track, then turning right to the deer viewing platform.

2 When you've finished deer spotting head down **Bolderwood Hill**, with the platform on your right, to follow the path with benches on your left and a red and blue post. This path veers left at the bottom and leads to a cross track.

3 Turn right and follow the path to a bench and another cross track.

4 Turn right and walk to a wider path, where you turn right again. This path curves round to meet another path.

5 Turn right and follow the track through the trees, crossing a cattle grid, with the landscape on the left opening up to give a lovely vista across the heathland. The deer sanctuary is now on your right, so there are lots of opportunities to spot deer here. The path leads gradually uphill, to cross a road and walk to the **Canadian Memorial**.

6 Walk past the memorial to cross a small parking area, then through a wooden gate on your right into woods. Ignore a grass path forking off on your left, and continue along a gravel path heading east.

7 When you come to post 102, turn right along a winding path through pine trees to post 144. Turn left at the cross track to post 145, where you turn right and head up between the trees, until you see the car park ahead of you.

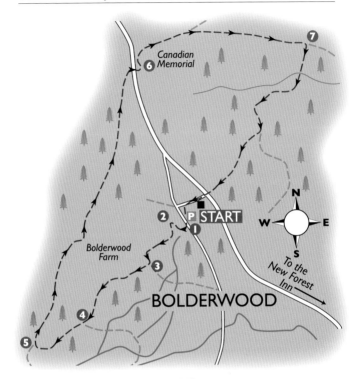

PLACES OF INTEREST NEARBY

The **New Forest Reptile Centre** (SO43 7GR) is home to rare snakes, lizards and adders. Outdoor 'pods' give you the opportunity to view them close up. Entry is free, but they suggest a donation to help cover their costs. It's open during school holidays and bank holidays. The **New Forest Heritage Centre** in Lyndhurst is open every day and is free to enter. It's packed with displays and activities and is the perfect spot for finding out about the history and traditions of the New Forest.

17 Rhinefield

4½ miles / 7 km

WALK HIGHLIGHTS

This walk starts by the shallow banks of Ober Water, before heading north across a classic New Forest landscape of grassland, heather and gorse, with plenty of opportunities to spot ponies as well as the occasional deer. Return along gravel tracks, before a stretch along a road famous for its towering conifers leads you back to the car park.

THE PUB

The Huntsman of Brockenhurst, Brockenhurst, SO42 7RH.
☎ 01590 622225 ⊕ www.thehuntsmanofbrockenhurst.com

THE WALK

1 Walk from the far end of the car park, heading away from the road and following the **Ober Water Trail** through tall trees. Continue along the path with the stream on your right until you come to a second footbridge.

2 Now turn left, following the wide path heading north, passing **Aldridge Hill Cottage** on your left. Just behind the cottage turn left along a gravel path, cross a small ditch then turn right along a wide

Guide to Hampshire & the New Forest Pub Walks

START & PARKING: The Forestry Commission Car Park at Puttles Bridge, just off Rhinefield Road. **Sat Nav:** SO42 7QB.

MAP: OS Explorer OL22 New Forest. **Grid Ref:** SU271029.

TERRAIN: Level walking and a good option for wet weather as half the walk uses flat gravel paths.

grassy path into the moorland, passing a no cycling sign on a post on the right. Walk ahead over this ancient landscape, with heather either side of the path. Cross a footbridge and continue on wide grassy paths between gorse bushes filled with tiny flowers in early summer. Cross another footbridge over **Fletchers Water**. Walk a short distance to a junction of grassy paths.

❸ At the Y-junction, take the option on the right, veering diagonally right on a wide grassy path, that narrows to raised gravel between the trees, before leading you to a fence. Turn right and walk with the fence on your left, then at the corner, head off veering diagonally to the left along a narrow grassy path between the heather, heading towards birch trees. Walk through the trees and you will see a footbridge ahead of you leading over **Highland Water**.

❹ Don't go as far as the bridge, instead turn left to follow a wide gravel path, popular with cyclists. Go through a wooden gate and stay on this path as it leads you through **Poundhill Enclosure**. Pass two cross tracks.

❺ At the third cross track, turn left, passing a warning sign for the ford. The path joins a gravel track and you turn left, shortly crossing the ford over a footbridge. The track leads you through **Fletchers Hill Enclosure** until eventually you come to **Rhinefield Road**.

❻ Turn left and walk roadside, admiring the tall pine trees. Pass **Rhinefield House Hotel** on your right, then look out for a barrier gate on your left. Go through the gate to follow a sandy track under the shade of the trees. Turn right at a hairpin bend, and walk with a fence on your left. Follow the fence as it turns to the left, then follow the path as it weaves through the trees, with the road on your right, until you see the car park ahead.

PLACES OF INTEREST NEARBY

Blackwater Arboretum
is the perfect spot for tree
lovers to explore, with a
stunning collection of trees
from around the world.
Head north along
Rhinefield
Drive to the
Blackwater
car park.
For car
lovers,

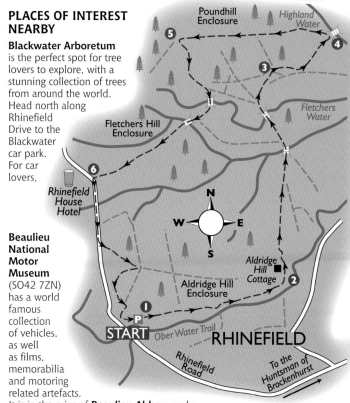

**Beaulieu
National
Motor
Museum**
(SO42 7ZN)
has a world
famous
collection
of vehicles,
as well
as films,
memorabilia
and motoring
related artefacts.

It is in the ruins of **Beaulieu Abbey**, and a
short walk along the river takes you to nearby **Buckler's Hard**, where
ships for Nelson's fleet were once built.

18 Burley

5 miles / 8 km

WALK HIGHLIGHTS

The route crosses heathland to Burley village, then back through woods and over streams to follow the old Southampton to Dorchester railway line. Burley is a delightful New Forest village, with plenty of options for refreshments in the middle of the walk. It was also once a famous haunt for smugglers, a hidden cellar with pistols and coins was discovered during renovations at the 16th-century Queens Head.

THE PUB

Queens Head, Burley, BH24 4AB.
☎ 01425 403423
⊕ www.chefandbrewer.com/pubs/hampshire/queens-head

THE WALK

1 Leave the car park and cross the road with care. Turn right and follow the wide grassy verge. Just before the sign for Burley, veer left along a narrow grassy path into **Church Moor**. The path leads diagonally away from the road to **Long Pond**.

2 Turn right by the pond to follow the path ahead across the moor. As you walk the scenery opens up with panoramic views across classic New Forest landscape. Stay on the track heading north.

START & PARKING: Burbush Car Park just off Pound Lane. **Sat Nav:** BH24 4EF.

MAP: OS Explorer OL22 New Forest. **Grid Ref:** SU202017.

TERRAIN: Mainly level with a few short uphill sections. One short section along a sunken path will be muddy after rain.

❸ After ½ mile, as the path leads uphill, look out for telegraph poles on your right. Here you turn right along a narrower sandy path. The path leads steeply uphill, past young pine trees and gorse, then under trees to **Castle Hill Lane**. Turn left along this track, walking under oak trees to a cross track and a 'no through road' sign. Turn right and walk along this wider track, passing **Castletop House** on your right. Continue ahead, by the side of a barrier gate, then along a path with fields on your left and a fence on your right. This path turns into a sunken path between trees for a short stretch, then a track leading to **Ringwood Road**.

❹ Turn right, heading towards Burley, and follow the pavement on the right of the road, until you come to a footpath sign. Here the path crosses the road, then follows a path through a gate and above the road, with paddocks on your left. Go through a gate, then cross the road with care.

❺ Follow the pavement through **Burley** to the war memorial, then cross the road with care by the **Burley Inn** and walk up **Chapel Lane** to the **Queens Head**. At the pub, cross the road and walk up **School Hill** for a short distance. Just past the school warning sign, cross and follow the narrow path through the trees, leading diagonally away from the road through oak trees to a gravel track.

❻ Turn right and walk a short distance to a Y-junction. Take the path on the left, signed Moorhill House Hotel. After about 20 metres, look out for the path on your left, with holly bushes either side. Turn left along this path and head through the woods, then back onto the moorland. You will see a cross path in front of you with a small car park on your left.

❼ Turn right and follow the path away from the car park to a wider path. Turn right and follow this path down **Shappen Bottom**, with **Turf Hill**

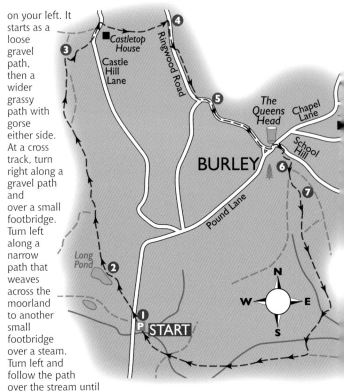

on your left. It starts as a loose gravel path, then a wider grassy path with gorse either side. At a cross track, turn right along a gravel path and over a small footbridge. Turn left along a narrow path that weaves across the moorland to another small footbridge over a steam. Turn left and follow the path over the stream until you come to the former track bed of the Southampton to Dorchester railway line. Turn right then right at the end to return to the car park.

PLACES OF INTEREST NEARBY

Liberty's Owl, Raptor and Reptile Centre is 3 miles west of Burley. They have a large collection of birds of prey.

19 Lymington Salt Marshes

4½ miles / 7 km

WALK HIGHLIGHTS

Lymington is a quaint coastal market town with winding cobble lanes, independent shops and cafés, making it an excellent base for this coastal walk. Starting by the marina, follow the seawall with stunning views across the mudflats and saltwater marshes. For 700 years this was the centre of a salt working industry, and is now the breeding ground for a variety of wading birds. There are benches dotted along the path if you want to take a moment to admire the open skies and sea views. The Mayflower is a large, nautically-themed pub with a fantastic beer garden overlooking the marina. It's well worth visiting at the end of the walk and serves good food. You could easily extend this walk by following the Solent Way to Keyhaven and the Gun Inn, then back across Keyhaven and Pennington Marshes.

THE PUB

The Mayflower, Lymington, SO41 3QD.
☎ 01590 672160   ⊕ www.themayflowerlymington.co.uk

Guide to Hampshire & the New Forest Pub Walks

START & PARKING: Bath Road Amenity Car Park in Lymington.
Sat Nav: SO41 3QF.

MAP: OS Explorer OL22 New Forest. **Grid Ref:** SZ333950.

TERRAIN: Level walking along well maintained paths and lanes.

THE WALK

1 Cross the car park towards the **Solent** and turn right to follow the public footpath, passing the **Baths** then yachts in the **marina**. Follow the signed footpath into **Lymington Yacht Haven** and half way across the car park, opposite shops, turn left to follow the **Solent Way** past a blue lamp post and along a roped walkway. Keep in the same direction along a gravel path through reed beds with **Normandy Marsh** on your right. At a footpath post, don't go down the steps, instead turn left. Walk along a raised path with views across the Solent, passing an information board about the Salterns.

2 At **Moses Dock**, turn left through the gates and over the bridge, then turn right and down steps by a strip of water with **Oxey Marsh** on your left. Note: to extend the walk, turn left here and follow the sea path round **Oxey Marsh** and along the coast to **Keyhaven**.

3 Turn right through the gates, following the **Solent Way**, then right through a gap in the fence to follow a gravel path in front of a house, then a dilapidated barn. Stay on the **Solent Way**, now following a shady path, pass a bungalow and continue ahead, passing **Salterns Sailing Club**. The path ends at a bend in the road, by a wooden post.

4 Turn right, to return to **Eight Acre Pond**, following a narrow footpath. Veer left through a kissing gate, then ahead to a bench in front of **Maiden Dock**. Now turn left, retracing your steps back along the sea path. Look out for a small black sign for cyclists, where you turn left down a path and through a gate, heading away from the sea.

5 Go through a gate onto **Normandy Lane** and turn right. Follow this quiet winding lane until you come to a footpath sign on your right. Walk along a gravel path past the reed beds of the nature reserve. Then turn right and follow the roped path back through **Lymington Yacht Haven** and retrace your steps past the yachts to your car.

PLACES OF INTEREST NEARBY

A well-deserved trip on an open top double decker bus with the **New Forest Tour** is a good way to appreciate the countryside after a long walk. There are three routes, and you can hop on and off the bus at various spots and switch between the routes. It runs from June to September: www. morebus. co.uk/ about-NFT. **St Barbe Museum and Art Gallery** explores the

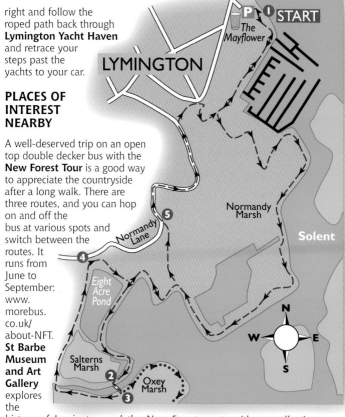

history of Lymington and the New Forest coast, with art collections and hands-on displays to keep everyone entertained. The collections represent life along the coast of the New Forest, including smugglers, salt makers and boat builders: stbarbe-museum.org.uk

20 Historic Portsmouth

3 miles / 4.8 km

WALK HIGHLIGHTS

The seafront at Portsmouth is a fascinating place to explore, with cobbled streets filled with naval history, sea views, and pubs on every corner. The walk starts at Gunwharf Quays, which has been immaculately restored with designer shops at one end and the seafront at the other. The walk follows part of the Millennium Promenade, enjoying impressive views across the harbour in Old Portsmouth. You also explore Capstan Square, named after the capstan that was kept here and used to raise a chain across the harbour entrance to block enemy ships from entering. The high grass bank by Royal Garrison Church was also originally defensive, built to defend Portsmouth from attack. The Georgian Old Customs House on Gunwharf Quays is an impressive building and part of the city's maritime history, once being the administrative headquarters for HMS *Vernon*. Now you can sit outside to people watch, or in the spacious interior. It serves an excellent lunchtime menu with good quality food and is well worth a visit.

THE PUB

The Old Customs House, Portsmouth, PO1 3TY.
☎ 023 92832333 ⊕ www.theoldcustomshouse.com

START & PARKING: Start at Gunwharf Quays where there is a car park for the shopping outlet or park nearby in the Harbour Car Park on Havant Street. **Sat Nav:** PO1 3HA.

MAP: OS Explorer OL29 Isle of Wight. **Grid Ref:** SU631002.

TERRAIN: Pavements with some steps.

THE WALK

1 Walk down **Gunwharf Quays** to the waterfront, stopping to admire **Spinnaker Tower** and the yachts in the harbour. Turn left, cross the footbridge and follow the **Millennium Promenade** – a chain motif set into the pavement. Cross the road and follow the sign towards 'Old Portsmouth'. Turn right down **Feltham Row**, with **Camber Quay** on your right, first inhabited as a fishing settlement by the Normans in the 12th century.

2 Turn right at the end of the road onto **Broad Street** and follow the **Millennium Promenade**. There are craft shops on the opposite side of the road and through the arch is a stretch of pebbly beach. Walk down **Broad Street** to **Portsmouth Point** and **Bath Square**, with impressive views back towards the harbour, **Spinnaker Tower** and **HMS** _Warrior_. This would once have been a dangerous spot for young men to sit, as it was the main meeting point for the press gang.

3 Pass the **Spice Island Inn** on your left, and the **Still and West pub** on your right, and continue following the **Millennium Promenade** to **Capstan Square** and the **Round Tower**. Go up the staircase and enjoy a fantastic view across the harbour as you walk along the raised pathway.

4 Look out for a statue of **Nelson** down on your left, and walk down the slope past the statue to see **Royal Garrison Church**, built in the early 13th century as a hospital for travellers and pilgrims. It unfortunately lost its roof in the Second World War from bomb damage and there is a conservation project going on to protect the building for the future. Past the church, head up the steps on your right, to return to the sea view. Just before a cannon, turn left and head down the slope and cross **Pembroke Gardens** via a narrow footpath, to **Pembroke Road**.

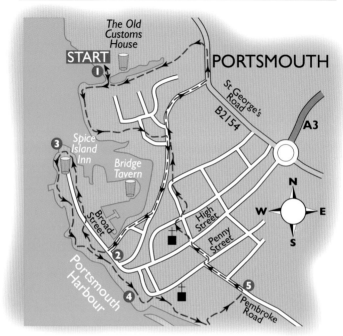

5 Turn left and follow the road, crossing **Penny Street** and **High Street** to the cathedral. Walk down **Lombard Street**, with the cathedral on your left. You could take a small detour by cutting through the tranquil 'Garden of Rest'. Then continue ahead and you will presently find yourself back on the millennial promenade on **Regency Court**. Follow it for a short while, but instead of turning left, keep ahead, following the sign to **Gunwharf Quays**. Turn left to return to the start.

PLACES OF INTEREST NEARBY
Portsmouth Historic Dockyard is home to the Mary Rose Museum, as well as other museums and historic ships.